ROBOTS AND ROBOTICS

# MEDICAL ROBOTS

## DANIEL R. FAUST

**PowerKiDS** press

New York

Published in 2017 by The Rosen Publishing Group, Inc.
29 East 21st Street, New York, NY 10010

First Edition

Editor: Caitie McAneney
Book Design: Reann Nye

Photo Credits: Cover FRANK PERRY/AFP/Getty Images; p. 4 science photo/Shutterstock.com; p. 5 Ociacia/Shutterstock.com; p. 6 ChinaFotoPress/Visual China Group/Getty Images; p. 7 RJ Sangosti/ Getty Images; p. 8 https://commons.wikimedia.org/wiki/File:Laproscopic_Surgery_Robot.jpg; p. 9 © iStockphoto.com/3alexd; p. 10 https://commons.wikimedia.org/wiki/File:Unimate_500_PUMA_ Deutsches_Museum.jpg; p. 13 https://commons.wikimedia.org/wiki/File:Cmglee_Cambridge_Science_ Festival_2015_da_Vinci_console.jpg; p. 14 Rick Madonik/Getty Images; p. 15 Andy Tullis /AP Images; pp. 16, 27 Boston Globe/Getty Images; p. 17 Peter Macdiarmid/Getty Images News/Getty Images; p. 18 Michael Courtney/Shutterstock.com; p. 19 Mark Runnacles/Getty Images News/Getty Images; p. 21 Jeff J Mitchell/Getty Images News/Getty Images; p. 22 https://commons.wikimedia.org/wiki/ File:Pharmacy_provides_exceptional_patient_care_150417-F-MI136-196.jpg; p. 23 STAN HONDA/ AFP/Getty Images; p. 25 Bloomberg/Getty Images; p. 26 Dmitry Kalinovsky/Shutterstock.com; p. 29 Lightspring/Shuttersrtock.com; p. 30 Coneyl Jay/Stone/Getty Images.

Cataloging-in-Publication Data

Names: Faust, Daniel R.
Title: Medical robots / Daniel R. Faust.
Description: New York : PowerKids Press, 2017. | Series: Robots and robotics | Includes index.
Identifiers: ISBN 9781499421750 (pbk.) | ISBN 9781499421774 (library bound) | ISBN 9781499421767 (6 pack)
Subjects: LCSH: Robotic in medicine-Juvenile literature. | Robotics-Juvenile literature.
Classification: LCC TJ211.2 F38 2017 | DDC 629.8'92-d23

Manufactured in the United States of America

CPSIA Compliance Information: Batch #BS16PK: For Further Information contact Rosen Publishing, New York, New York at 1-800-237-9932

# CONTENTS

MAKING LIFE EASIER. . . . . . . . . . . . . . . . . . . . . . . .4

HOW ROBOTS WORK. . . . . . . . . . . . . . . . . . . . . .6

SURGICAL ROBOTS . . . . . . . . . . . . . . . . . . . .8

OPERATING ROOM ROBOTS. . . . . . . . . . . . . . .12

THE ROBOT WILL SEE YOU NOW . . . . . . . . . .14

ROBOTS AND RECOVERY . . . . . . . . . . . . . . .16

BIONIC BODIES. . . . . . . . . . . . . . . . . . . . . . . .18

ROBOT PHARMACIES . . . . . . . . . . . . . . . . . . .22

ROBOT OR ORDERLY?. . . . . . . . . . . . . . . . . . .24

KEEPING THINGS CLEAN . . . . . . . . . . . . . . . 26

WORLD'S SMALLEST ROBOTS. . . . . . . . . . . .28

WHAT WILL TOMORROW BRING? . . . . . . . . . .30

GLOSSARY. . . . . . . . . . . . . . . . . . . . . . . . . . .31

INDEX . . . . . . . . . . . . . . . . . . . . . . . . . . . . . . .32

WEBSITES . . . . . . . . . . . . . . . . . . . . . . . . . . . .32

gine a world where robots work alongside doctors
atients the best health care. Imagine a robot
t fits inside your body to perform an operation.
as aren't impossible. In fact, this kind of robot
gy is already being developed and used today.
ots often replace people in situations that are
e or boring for a human worker. They can work
and perform the same task perfectly over and over.
amazing **precision** makes them great workers,
y in hospitals and other health-care settings.

Hospitals of the future may be filled with advanced robots working together to help patients.

Today, some robots perform important surgeries, while others deliver medication and clean hospital rooms. Some robots are even used to replace lost limbs. They have great potential to save lives.

# HOW ROBOTS WORK

Engineers build medical robots with a specific task in mind. However, even these robots have basic robot parts.

A robot's sensors gather information about its surroundings. Some robots only have simple motion detectors, but others have video cameras and microphones that help them "see" and "hear." The controller processes the information gathered from a robot's sensors. A robot's controller is like its brain. It's programmed with information it needs to perform the tasks it was designed to perform.

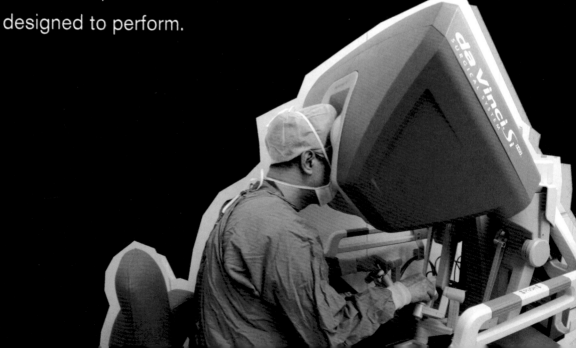

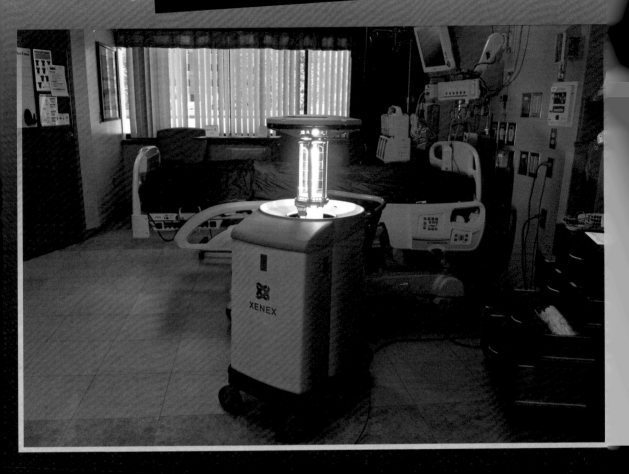

This hospital cleaning robot has a controller, sensors, actuators, and effectors.

The controller also operates effectors and actuators, which are a robot's moving parts. Effectors allow robots to perform specific tasks. They serve as the robot's arms and hands. Actuators are motors that make the different parts

# SURGICAL ROBOTS

You may have seen pictures of robots used in factories. These giant machines cut, drill, assemble, or paint many different kinds of products. It's hard to imagine these huge robots in the operating room, but robots are becoming more common in medical settings every year.

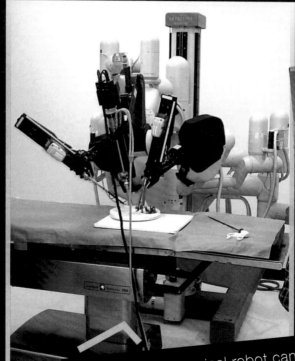

The arms of a surgical robot can access the body parts being operated on more easily than other methods.

Robots are used in operating rooms around the world for the same reasons they're used in factories. Surgical robots can be precise and efficient. They're capable of performing difficult tasks the same way every time. A major benefit of surgical robots is that they can perform procedures in a much less **invasive** way with less harm to the patient. Surgical robots can often perform surgeries with smaller **incisions** than those made by human surgeons alone.

There are two kinds of surgical robots in use. Some robots are operated **remotely** by a surgeon. The surgeon performs all the normal movements for an operation, but the robot's arms carry out the actual surgery. Computer-controlled surgical robots are a little different. These surgical robots are controlled by programs and commands a surgeon enters into a computer.

In 1985, the Unimation PUMA 560 was used during brain surgery with great success. This is considered by many to be the first surgical procedure carried out with the help of a robot. In 2000, the da Vinci Surgical System completely changed the medical world. It gave surgeons a 3-D view of the surgery site and the ability to control surgical arms.

Using robots for medical purposes is a fairly new practice, beginning in the 1980s. Learn more about the history of medical robots!

# TIMELINE OF MEDICAL ROBOTS

**1985**

The PUMA 560 becomes the first robot to assist during a surgical procedure.

**1988**

The PROBOT, developed at Imperial College London, is used to perform a surgery.

**1990s**

The National Aeronautics and Space Administration (NASA) and the Stanford Research Institute develop robots that can carry out the actions of surgeons from a distance.

**1992**

The first ROBODOC system assists a surgeon with a hip surgery.

**1994**

The AESOP voice-activated robotic system is approved for use during surgical procedures.

**1998**

The Zeus Robotic Surgical System is used for its first surgical procedure on a human.

**2000**

The da Vinci Surgical System is approved for use in American hospitals.

**2001**

The SOCRATES system is approved. Also, the first transatlantic surgery is performed by a doctor and robot on opposite sides

# OPERATING ROOM ROBOTS

One of the most common robots used in operating rooms around the world is the da Vinci Surgical System. The da Vinci system allows surgeons to perform delicate procedures remotely. The system has three robotic arms. Two of the arms respond to the surgeon's left and right arm movements. A surgeon uses a separate control **console** to guide the arms during surgery. This is similar to the Zeus Robotic Surgical System, which was first used in 1998, but is no longer commonly used.

The da Vinci system uses an endoscope, which is a thin tube with a tiny camera and light at the end. The Zeus system used AESOP, which was a voice-controlled camera system attached to Zeus's third robotic arm. AESOP could provide real-time video of the area the surgeon was operating on.

# HOW DOES REMOTE SURGERY WORK?

## STEP ONE

Nurses get the patient ready for surgery. The patient arrives at the operating room.

## STEP TWO

A bedside camera relays images of the patient to the surgeon's control station.

## STEP THREE

The surgeon uses controls to perform the motions of the procedure.

## STEP FOUR

Robot arms at the side of the patient's bed repeat the surgeon's motions and perform the surgery.

The control console of the da Vinci Surgical System provides the surgeon controlling the robot arms with a 3-D image of the area being operated on

# THE ROBOT WILL SEE YOU NOW

Telepresence is the use of **virtual reality** technology to participate in something from a different place. Doctors can use this technology to provide medical assistance to patients even when they're miles apart. These robots move through the halls of today's hospitals. They help doctors **diagnose** patients from afar, which is helpful when patients have diseases, or illnesses, that spread easily. These robots can also be sent to parts of the world where people don't have access to medical care.

## OUTBREAK!

The military uses robots to handle dangerous materials, such as explosives, while keeping human soldiers at a safe distance. Doctors can use robots in a similar way. In 2014 and 2015, there was an outbreak of a dangerous disease called Ebola. Ebola is deadly and spreads easily, so officials considered using robots to reduce human contact with infected patients. Robots can clean patients' rooms and retrieve dirty laundry. This kind of remote-controlled robot technology could help keep doctors and nurses safe during future outbreaks.

A great deal of thought goes into designing robots that doctors can operate from a distance. The doctor needs a robot's camera to have a full range of movement so they can **accurately** examine and diagnose the patient.

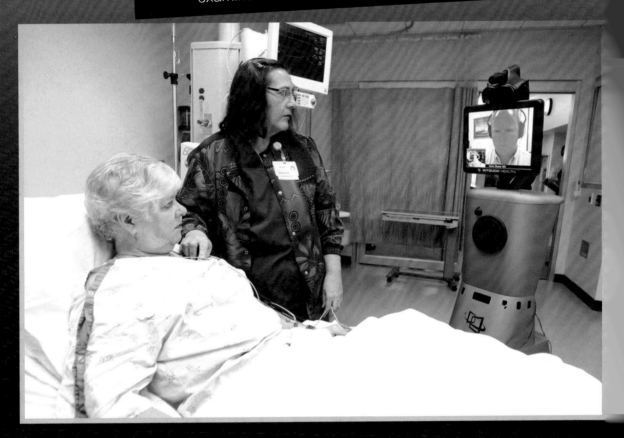

Flying robots, commonly called drones, are also used for medical purposes. Drones deliver medication, food, and water to people in hard-to-reach places. Flying drones may someday also carry important equipment and supplies to

# ROBOTS AND RECOVERY

Robots are also used to help patients recover after surgery. Many patients require **physical therapy**, which helps them strengthen muscles and regain movement. Some robots are used to assist human physical therapists. A common use for robots is helping patients move and therefore strengthen their muscles. For example, a robot might help a person gradually work to move their arm after it's injured in an accident.

## REWALK

ReWalk was the first exoskeleton cleared by the Federal Drug Administration (FDA) for personal use in the United States. It's designed to allow its user to walk around both at home and in the community. ReWalk is also used in therapy settings to help people who are paralyzed exercise their lower body. Users can walk, turn, and stand upright. The development of exoskeletons like the ReWalk gives people who are paralyzed hope that they'll walk again one day.

Claire Lomas, who is paralyzed from the waist down, walked a marathon in 2012 using a ReWalk.

Exoskeletons are a type of wearable robot, and they have several medical uses. They're used to help **stroke** survivors strengthen weakened muscles and relearn how to move certain body parts. Exoskeletons are also used to help paralyzed patients, or those who are unable to move their limbs. Some hospitals have a patient wear an exoskeleton and walk on a treadmill to strengthen their muscles.

# BIONIC BODIES

If you like science fiction, you might know the words "bionic" and "cyborg." Bionic means having artificial, usually electronic, body parts. A cyborg is a person who may have special abilities because of bionic devices built into their body. Thanks to advances in robotics and medicine, science fiction is quickly becoming science fact.

The claw at the end of this man's prosthetic arm is only capable of simple gripping. However, the advanced prosthetic hand on page 19 can function more like a real hand.

Prostheses are artificial devices used to replace missing body parts. They've been around for thousands of years. Throughout most of history, simple wooden or metal prostheses were used to replace hands, arms, and legs. Simple prostheses were made mostly for appearance and couldn't function like real body parts.

As technology advanced, prostheses started to be able to perform the basic functions of the body parts they were replacing. Prosthetic hands went from simple hooks

The i-Limb robotic hand is one of the most advanced prosthetic hands. It has fingers that can move individually like a real hand. One day, prosthetic hands may advance further to give their owner a sense of touch.

In 2003, a project began to develop advanced prostheses for veterans returning from war without limbs. The result was the BiOM by iWalk. This prosthesis is a close copy of a functioning human leg, ankle, and foot.

Advanced prostheses, such as the i-Limb and the iWalk BiOM, use signals from the surrounding muscles and **nervous system**. This allows the patient to control them like a natural limb. In 2014, the FDA approved a new type of prosthetic arm called the DEKA Arm System. It is the first prosthetic arm controlled by muscle movements and electrical signals.

## BIOHACKING

Biohacking is when a person implants, or inserts, electronic or mechanical hardware in themselves to improve their abilities or give them new abilities. Some people have magnets, compasses, antennas, or tracking devices in their bodies. Biohackers aren't replacing their natural body parts with robotics just yet. However, many of the principles behind biohacking are similar to those used by the medical community when developing prosthetic robots.

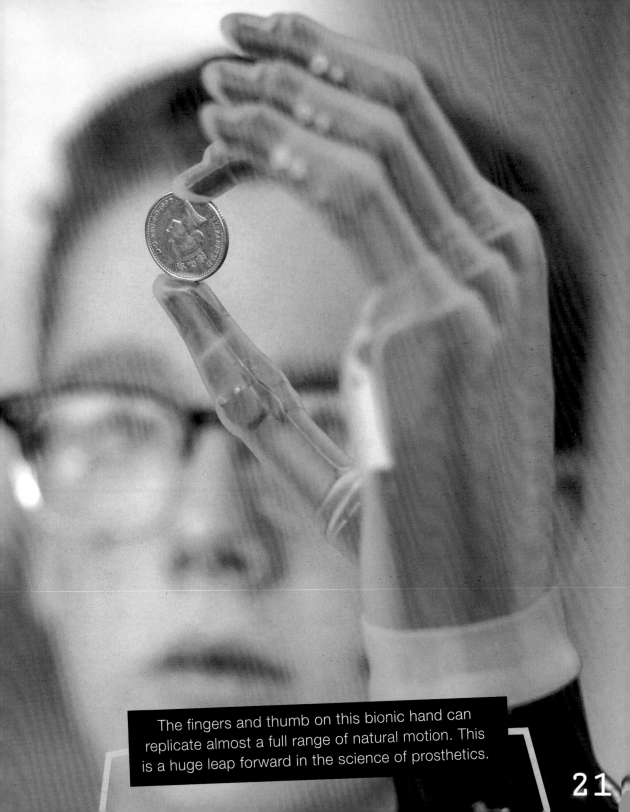

The fingers and thumb on this bionic hand can replicate almost a full range of natural motion. This is a huge leap forward in the science of prosthetics.

# ROBOT PHARMACIES

Robots are sometimes used in factories and warehouses for their ability to pick up and pack products. The same ability makes robots perfect for work in hospitals and pharmacies, or drugstores. When it comes to dispensing, or giving, medication to patients, precision is important. Too little medication and the patient may not recover, but too much might harm or kill them.

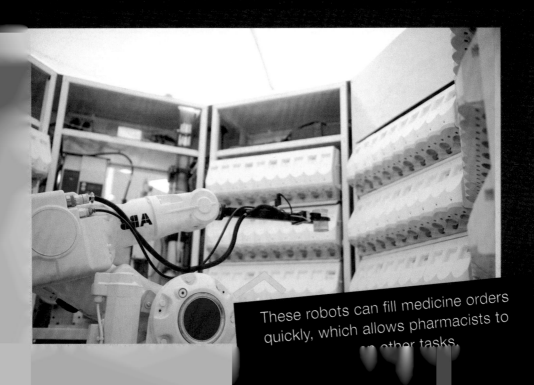

These robots can fill medicine orders quickly, which allows pharmacists to on other tasks.

Robot dispensing systems are being used in hospitals and commercial pharmacies around the world. These machines are capable of sorting and dispensing different pills. Some systems will even print and apply labels to medicine bottles. Human pharmacists are still needed to inspect each prescription as well as clean, refill, and

# ROBOT OR ORDERLY?

It takes a lot of work for a hospital to run smoothly. Doctors, nurses, and pharmacists are all important, but orderlies perform much of the day-to-day work done in hospitals. Orderlies are the men and women who bring patients their food, change bedsheets, keep things clean, and make sure the patients are as comfortable as possible.

In 2015, a new hospital in San Francisco, California, started using robot orderlies called TUGs. These slow-moving robots roll through the hospital, delivering food and medications. They also carry laundry and trash from patients' rooms. TUGs navigate using the hospital's **Wi-Fi** signals and use onboard sensors to avoid people and objects. Each one travels about 12 miles (19.3 km) a day!

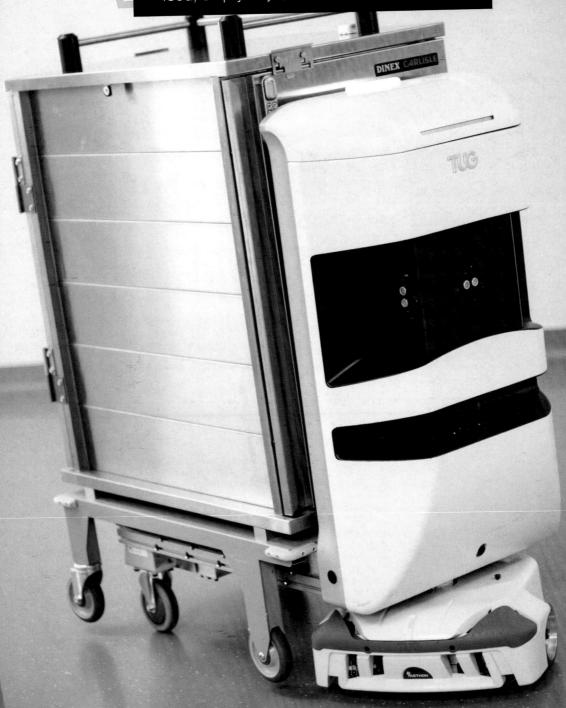

The cart carried by a TUG can be used to carry food, empty trays, medications, and laundry.

25

Hospital workers are at risk of catching whatever [dise]ases patients bring into the hospital. Patients are also [at ri]sk of catching new diseases. Patients' immune systems [are] already busy attacking the illnesses they already have, [whi]ch makes it hard to fight other illnesses. Also, any [inci]sions from surgery are open doors for germs. That's why [hosp]itals need to be as clean as possible.

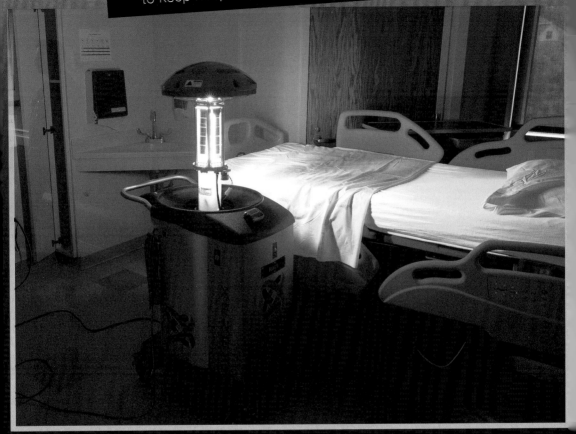

Germs are everywhere. Hospitals need to be extremely clean to keep patients from getting infected. Robots like this one use ultraviolet light to keep hospitals as germ-free as possible.

Anyone can go out and buy a robot vacuum cleaner like a Roomba, but hospitals require something a little more powerful. Some robots release a mist of chemicals into the air to **disinfect** an area. Some robots use ultraviolet, or UV, light to kill potentially dangerous germs.

# WORLD'S SMALLEST ROBOTS

Microrobotics and nanorobotics are branches of robotics that deal with very small robots. Insect-sized microrobots, such as the ViRob, measure only millimeters, or fractions of an inch, in length. That's small enough to crawl through the human body. The ViRob uses its tiny arms to move through a patient's body, delivering drugs to the right body parts and sending images to doctors.

Nanorobotics may be the future of medicine. Engineers are working on ways to design and build robots that are no larger than a single cell or molecule. Today, an infection might be treated with weeks of antibiotics. Nanorobots could get rid of harmful germs inside a patient in minutes. These microscopic robots could even perform surgery at the cellular level by removing or repairing diseased and damaged cells.

Although nanorobots aren't yet a reality, some scientists see a future where they could be injected directly into a patient to fight disease and repair injuries.

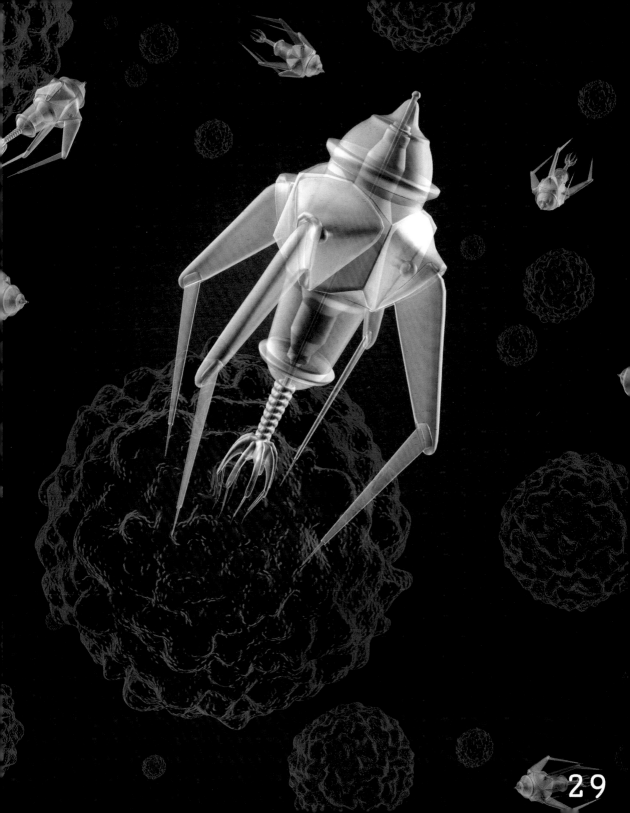

# WHAT WILL TOMORROW BRING?

The last 30 years have seen many advances in the field of medical robotics. Today, robots assist during surgical procedures, dispense medication, and keep hospitals neat and orderly. Robots are even being used to replace missing arms and legs.

It's unlikely that we'll ever see a hospital staffed entirely by robot doctors and nurses. It's much more likely that the hospitals of tomorrow will feature doctors and nurses working alongside robots and robot orderlies. Robotic prostheses and wearable technology such as exoskeletons may someday function just like natural body parts. This could make physical disabilities a thing of the past. Nanorobots could be used to repair and replace damaged cells, helping us stay healthy. Robots may be the future of

# GLOSSARY

**accurate:** Free from mistakes.

**console:** A device by which an operator can control and monitor another device.

**diagnose:** To recognize a disease by signs and symptoms.

**disinfect:** To clean something in a way that kills all germs.

**incision:** A cut made into the body during surgery.

**invasive:** Involving entry into the living body.

**nervous system:** The system of nerves that sends messages for controlling feeling and movement between the brain and body.

**physical therapy:** The treatment of a disease or an injury using physical methods, such as exercises.

**precision:** The quality of being exact or accurate.

**remote:** Controlled indirectly or from a distance.

**stroke:** A sudden blockage or break of a blood vessel in the brain.

**virtual reality:** An artificial world made of images and sounds that is affected by the actions of the person who is experiencing it.

**Wi-Fi:** The wireless network technology that connects computers and other electronic devices to each other and

# INDEX

**A**
actuators, 7
AESOP, 11, 12

**B**
BiOM, 20
bionic, 18, 21

**C**
controllers, 6, 7
cyborg, 18

**D**
da Vinci Surgical System, 10, 11,
    12, 13
DEKA Arm System, 20
drones, 15

**E**
Ebola, 14
effectors, 7
endoscope, 12
exoskeletons, 16, 17, 30

**F**
FDA (Federal Drug Administration),
    16, 20

**I**
i-Limb, 20, 21

**M**
microrobotics, 28

**N**
nanorobotics, 28, 30
NASA (National Aeronautics and
    Space Administration), 11

**P**
pharmacies, 22, 23
physical therapy, 16
PROBOT, 11
prostheses, 18, 19, 20, 21, 30

**R**
ReWalk, 16, 17
ROBODOC, 11

**S**
sensors, 6, 7, 24
SOCRATES, 11
surgical robots, 8, 9, 10

**T**
telepresence, 14
TUG, 24, 25

**U**
Unimation PUMA 560, 10, 11

**V**
ViRob, 28

**Z**
Zeus Robotic Surgical System, 11, 12

# WEBSITES

Due to the changing nature of Internet links, PowerKids Press has developed an
online list of websites related to the subject of this book. This site is updated regularly.
Please use this link to access the list: www.powerkidslinks.com/rar/medic